A book
is a present you can open
again and again.

THIS BOOK BELONGS TO

_____

FROM

_____

Learn 'n Do

WAYS WITH WORDS

Illustrated by Rick Incrocci

World Book, Inc.
a Scott Fetzer company
Chicago London Sydney Toronto

Dear Parent,

You may want to join your child in making some of the projects in this book, or be present in the room where your child is working. If you are with your child, you can lend a hand, answer questions that may arise, and make sure that your child is using materials appropriately.

Have fun!
The Editors of World Book

Printed in the United States of America
ISBN 0-7166-1613-0
Library of Congress Catalog Card No. 91-65520

C/IC

Cover design by Rosa Cabrera

Oday Ouyay Eakspay Igpay Atinlay?

Pig Latin is a code language in which real words are changed according to a few simple rules.

Rule 1

When a word begins with a vowel (a,e,i,o,u), add "way" to the end of the word. So, in pig Latin, "I am eating an apple" is written like this:

Iway amway eatingway anway appleway.

Rule 2

When a word begins with a single consonant, place the first letter at the end of the word and then add "ay" after the letter. In pig Latin, you'd write "Give me my book back" like this:

Ivegay emay ymay ookbay ackbay.

IVEGAY EMAY YMAY OOKBAY ACKBAY.

What can you say in pig Latin?

Morse Code Messages

The Morse code was invented by Samuel Morse. It is made up of long and short sounds that are written out as dots (. . .) and dashes (– – –). These sounds are used to send messages by shortwave radio. Here is the Morse code alphabet:

You will need:

a friend
paper
pencil
stick
can
whistle

A	B	C	D	E	F	G
•—	—•••	—•—•	—••	•	••—•	——•

H	I	J	K	L	M	N
••••	••	•———	—•—	•—••	——	—•

O	P	Q	R	S	T	U
———	•——•	——•—	•—•	•••	—	••—

V	W	X	Y	Z
•••—	•——	—••—	—•——	——••

1. First, print a short message on a piece of paper. Then have your friend take some blank paper and a pencil and stand a few feet (about a meter) away from you.

4

2. Now use a stick and a can to send your message by Morse code. Tap the stick against the side of the can to sound out a dash. *Or*, use a whistle to send your message: a short toot can be a dot, a longer blow can be a dash.

3. Be sure to pause a few seconds between each letter. Pause a few more seconds between words.

4. As you tap out or whistle your message, have your friend use the Morse code to figure out and write down the message.

5. After you're finished, compare your original message with the one your friend decoded. Do they match? Now ask your friend to send a message to you.

Now You See It;

Here's how to write an invisible message.

Invisible Writing

1. Pour some lemon juice into a bowl. Then dip a toothpick into the juice and write a message on a piece of paper. You will have to keep dipping the toothpick in the juice after you write each letter. Use a lot of juice and make your letters good and thick. Let the lemon juice dry only slightly.

2. Now turn on a lamp and hold your paper up to the lighted bulb. As you move the paper in front of the bulb, you will be able to read your message. Be careful not to burn yourself or the paper!

Now You Don't

Hidden Writing

1. Hold a piece of paper under a running faucet until the paper is all wet.
2. Then place the wet paper on top of a kitchen counter or plastic-covered table.
3. Cover the wet paper with a dry piece of paper.
4. Now write your message on the dry paper with a ballpoint pen. Press down hard as you write.
5. Throw the dry paper away.
6. When the wet paper dries, the message will be invisible. To make the invisible message visible, wet the paper again.

MEET A

MEET ME AT NOON!

Read My Mind

Play a word game with your friend. Learn to ask questions in order to guess the identity of an unknown object or thing.

1. Think of an object or a thing such as a Frisbee. Don't tell your friend what you're thinking about. He or she has to ask questions in order to learn enough facts about the object to guess what it is. Here are some sample questions your friend can use. Your answers should be brief and specific. No fair asking directly what the object is!

2. Your friend gets to ask five questions and then should try to guess what you're thinking about. Let him or her have three guesses.

3. If the guesses are not correct, allow more questions, until he or she guesses correctly.

4. Now reverse the roles. Your friend thinks of an object or a thing and you ask the questions.

Questions

What is its shape?

What is it made of?

What do you do with it?

Who uses it?

What does it look like?

Answers

It's round and flat.
It's made of plastic.
You throw it.
People who are playing and having fun use it.
It looks like a flying saucer.

8

When I Went to the Store...

Here's a describing game for you to play with your friends or family.

1. Have everyone sit in a circle. Before the game can begin, the players must choose a category to shop for, such as food, clothes, or toys.

2. It is up to the first player to choose a noun, or thing, to "buy" from that category. If the category is food, the thing could be a peach, a muffin, a carrot, or any other food item. The first player then begins the game by saying, for example, "When I went to the store, I bought a peach."

3. The next player has to add a sentence that describes what the first player bought. For example: "It was pink, fuzzy, and juicy."

4. The third player has to add another sentence that tells how the noun or thing will be used. For example: "I'll eat it for breakfast."

5. Then the fourth player has to repeat all three sentences. "When I went to the store, I bought a peach. It was pink, fuzzy, and juicy. I'll eat it for breakfast."

6. If a player is unable to make up a sentence or cannot repeat all three sentences, the next player will be called on to do so.

Picture's Worth a Thousand Words

Native Americans used picture writing to write stories. These stories were painted on deer, antelope, and buffalo hides. Look at the pictures below. These are drawings Native Americans used to illustrate nouns (people, animals, things, and places), verbs, and adjectives. They could combine these drawings to write a story—a picture story.

Native American Picture Writing

 MAN   BROTHERS   HORSE  TURTLE BIRD   BEAR   DEER   SNAKE

 CLOUD   HOUSE   DAY   CORN   RAIN RAINBOW   TEEPEE SUN

 TREE   GRASS   MOUNTAINS   RIVER

 WALK   EAT   COME   HEAR   SEE   SPEAK

 STRONG   OLD

10

You will need:

brown paper bag
crayons

Below is the first sentence of a picture story. Can you find the symbols in the drawings and figure out what the sentence means?

Now make up your own stories using Native American picture writing. You may want to invent some of your own picture symbols.

1. Use picture symbols to write the stories on a brown paper bag (and pretend it's buffalo hide).
2. Now "tan" the hide by crumpling the paper.

Concrete Writing

You will need:

paper
pencil

1. Pick a noun: Then write down some words that tell about the noun. Now use the words to draw the shape of the noun. In the example at the left, words that tell what the sun looks like, how the sun feels, and what the sun does are used to draw the shape of the sun.

2. Pick another noun. Now draw an outline of its shape. Fill the shape with words that tell about the noun. In the example, words that tell about a dog are used to fill in its outline.

Top Ten Lists

You will need:

paper
pencil

Make lists of the following:

Ten things that could never happen
Ten things I do every day
Ten things that are tall
Ten things that smell sweet
Ten things I'll never tell anyone
Ten things I wish would happen
Ten things that taste good
Ten things in my closet
Ten things that feel hot
Ten things that feel soft

13

Lost and Found Zoo

Here's an alphabet game for
you to play with your friends and family.

1. The first player begins by
thinking of an animal and an
adjective describing it that
both start with the letter *a*
and then another animal and
adjective that both start with
the letter *b*.

2. Then the player uses the
words in the following
sentence: I'm an (*a* adjective/
noun), and I'm looking for a
(*b* adjective/noun). For
example, the player could
say: "I'm an awful alligator,
and I'm looking for a brave
bumblebee."

3. Now the next player repeats
the *b* adjective/noun part of
the sentence and adds a *c*
adjective/noun. For example:
"I'm a brave bumblebee, and
I'm looking for a crazy
coyote."

4. Continue to play the game
until you have gone through
the entire alphabet.

I'M A ROTTEN RACCOON, AND I'M LOOKING FOR A SILLY SEAL.

I'M A SILLY SEAL. AND I'M LOOKING FOR A TIMID TIGER...

Dancing Feet

Dancers put together different dance steps to make a dance. You can be a dancer, too.

You will need:

index cards
pencil

1. Write one action word on each index card. Write action words that could be used as dance steps, such as stretch, leap, slide, run, crawl, fall, and spin.

2. Shuffle the cards and turn them over, facedown.
3. Then turn three cards over, faceup, one next to the other.
4. Do whatever the cards say in the order they say to do it. You've just invented a new dance.
5. Now do the same dance steps in reverse order.

Face Your Feelings

MAD

Sometimes adjectives tell how people look and feel. Your face can show how you are feeling. An adjective can describe the look on your face.

SAD

1. Look in the mirror and make the following faces:

sad	tired	silly
smiling	ugly	mean
happy	mad	laughing

2. Make some more faces in the mirror. Think of some other adjectives to describe your faces.

LAUGHING

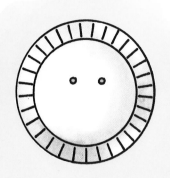

3. Then pick one of your favorite faces, such as a laughing face, and make a mask that looks like that face.

4. First, cut out holes in the paper plate where your eyes should go. Draw in eyelashes and eyebrows.

5. Then glue on yarn, buttons, and fabric scraps for the hair, nose, mouth, teeth, and ears.

6. Now tape the tube onto the back of the mask so that part of the tube can be used as a handle. Hold the mask in front of your face and look in the mirror again. Does your mask look like your favorite face?

YARN HAIR

BUTTON NOSE

MATERIAL SCRAPS FOR EARS & TEETH

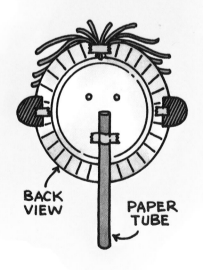

BACK VIEW

PAPER TUBE

Made-Up Menagerie

The imaginary animal in the picture is a *hipparoo.* It is part hippopotamus and part kangaroo.

You will need:

magazines or
    newspapers
scissors
construction paper
paste
crayons or markers
drawing paper
pencil

1. Cut out pictures of different animals from magazines or newspapers. Then cut the animals in half. Try different combinations of animal halves to make a new animal. Paste your new imaginary animal on a piece of construction paper.

2. If you like, you can draw a picture of an imaginary animal using parts of two or more real animals.

3. Now give your imaginary animal a name by putting together parts of the real animal names. Write out the new name below your picture or drawing.

4. Tell or write a story about the imaginary animal.

Word Rummy

You will need:

- magazines or newspapers
- scissors
- index cards
- glue or paste
- shoebox
- paper
- pencil

1. Cut out at least 50 words or groups of words from magazines and newspapers. Be sure you have lots of nouns, verbs, and adjectives.
2. Paste each word or word group on an index card.
3. Place the cards facedown in the shoebox.
4. Now pick ten cards out of the box, turn them over, and place them in front of you.
5. You need at least one noun and one verb to make a sentence. Can you make a sentence with your cards?
6. If you can't make a sentence, trade a card you can't use for a new one from the box.
7. When you can make a sentence, copy it onto a piece of paper. You can add a few words like *a, an,* or *the* if you have to.
8. When you have made a few sentences, use your best sentence as the first line of a story.

19

Word Chain

Make a word chain on a roll of adding machine tape or shelf paper. You can use any word to start. After the first word, the next word you write in the chain must be different from the word before it by one letter. It sounds harder than it is. Give it a try.

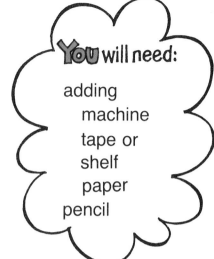

You will need:

adding machine tape or shelf paper
pencil

1. Follow these rules:
   a. You can add one letter to form the next word.   mat to math
   b. You can subtract one letter to form the next word.   mat to at
   c. You can replace one letter to form the next word.   mat to rat
   d. Don't repeat any words.

2. Try starting a word chain using the following words. Write each word on your paper tape and then add to the list. Remember to obey the four rules.

cat sat sap sip lip lit bit bite kite kit it if in pin pine fine find wind

3. Now make more chains. Start each chain with one of these words.

jump   best   mop   rust
pole   wide   tape   hope

4. Make your chains as long as you can.

Play a word chain game with a friend. Take turns adding words to the chain.

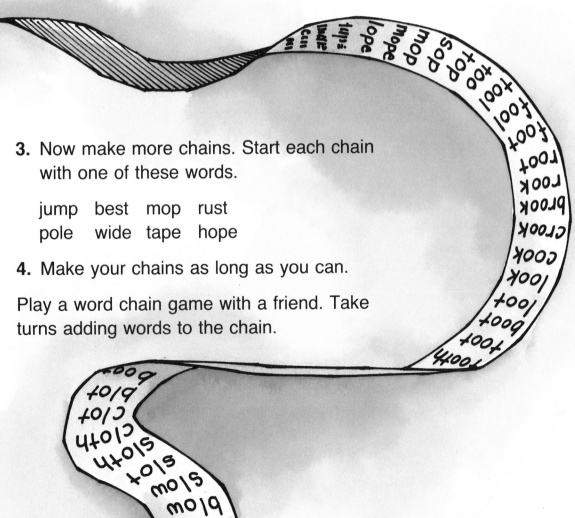

Make a sentence machine and you'll never be at a loss for words.

Sentence Machine

You will need:

an adult
cardboard
scissors
adding machine tape
pencil

1. Ask an adult to help you cut six slits out of a long piece of cardboard. Make the slits the same width as your adding machine tape. Then write the following on your sentence machine: "The (slit) monster (slit) into the (slit)." Make it look like the illustration below.

The		monster		into the	

2. Then cut three long pieces of paper from the roll of adding machine tape.
3. Make an adjective tape out of one of the tapes. Write these adjectives on the tape: large, round, sleepy, purple. Then add some of your own.

The sleepy monster slid into the mud

large round | skipped fell | soup cave lake

purple smelly | rolled drove | bed banana

4. Make a verb tape on another tape. Write these verbs on the tape: skipped, fell, slid, rolled, drove. Then add some of your own.

5. Make a noun tape on the remaining tape. Write these nouns on the tape: soup, cave, lake, mud, bed, banana. Then add some of your own.

6. Now thread the tapes into the slits in the cardboard. Insert the adjective tape into the first slit, the verb tape into the second slit, and the noun tape into the third slit. Pull the tapes up and down to make sentences.

23

This Is Your Life

You will need:
photos, souvenirs
pencil and paper
string
scissors
pins
tape
clothespins

You may not be famous—yet. But you have your own history. Remember when you took your first trip? Found a dog? Lost your first tooth? Went to school for the first time? Rode a bike? Met your baby sister? Moved to where you live now? All these events are part of your history. Here is how to record these events on your own special time line.

1. Collect photos and souvenirs from your past. If you like, you can also draw pictures of events in your life—a birthday party, a big vacation trip, the day you found a lost puppy, or any other important event.

2. Write the date on each item you collect or draw.

3. Cut off a piece of string long enough to hold your collection. Pin or tape the string along a wall of your room or between two walls.

4. Clip the items on the string according to the date on each of them. Start with a picture or souvenir from the time you were born. Continue clipping the items in order until you get to the items from the present time.

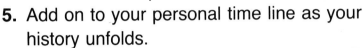

5. Add on to your personal time line as your history unfolds.

Family Flags

Every country has a flag. After you take your census, make a flag for each of the nations on your list.

You will need:

paper
scissors
a book or encyclopedia
   with pictures of flags
pencil
crayons or markers
straws
tape
clay

1. Find a picture of each flag you need in an encyclopedia.
2. Cut out rectangles of white paper.
3. Copy the patterns onto the paper in pencil.
4. Color the flags.

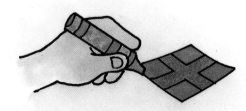

26

5. Tape each flag to the top third of a straw.

6. To make a stand for each flag stick the straw into a flat-bottomed lump of clay.

Census

Do you know what part of the world your ancestors lived in? Take a census (that's a fancy word for survey) to find out what countries your family, neighbors, and friends came from. Can you find these places on the map?

Country Cutouts

The ancestors of your family may have come from a lot of different countries. The people who live in some of those places may have a traditional way of dressing. Make some cutout people and dress them in a way that shows your heritage.

You will need:
white cardboard
pencil
crayons or markers
scissors
a book or encyclopedia that shows traditional costumes
paper

1. Outline your cutout people on the cardboard. Color in the skin, eyes, nose, and hair.
2. Cut out the people.
3. Look in the book for the costumes you want to make.

4. Copy and color the designs onto the paper. (Be sure the clothes will fit—use your cutouts as a guide.) Add tabs so you can fold the clothes around your cutout people.

5. Dress the cutout people in their traditional costumes.

⭐ **Amazing Fact**

All through history, people have worn clothes more for decoration than for covering the body. This is true even in cold climates.

City Planning

It's fun to make a box building. You may like it so much you will want to make a whole town.

You will need:

boxes and cartons
poster paint
brushes
scissors
crayons or markers
construction paper
paste or glue

1. Collect boxes and cartons of different shapes and sizes.

2. Pick one that would make a good building.

3. Paint the outside of the box.

4. Cut out spaces for the doors and windows. Get help if you need it.

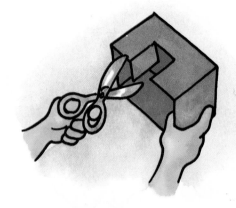

5. Draw doors and windows on the construction paper and cut them out. Be sure to make them the same size as the doors and windows you cut out of the box.

6. Glue one side of each door and window to your box building so they can open and close.

Make several buildings. Set them up to make a city. Create your own community with box buildings of all shapes. Try a milk carton house, a shoebox hospital. You might even try gluing two boxes together to make a skyscraper.

Special Delivery

You will need:

scissors   paper towels
warm water   stiff paper

Start your own stamp collection.
Just study the letters that come
to your house and save the
stamps you like.

1. Cut out the stamps from the
   envelopes.
2. Soak the stamps in a bowl of
   warm water.
3. When the stamps come
   loose, peel them from the
   paper.
4. Put the stamps on paper towels.
5. Let the stamps dry.
6. Glue the stamps to a piece of stiff paper
   any way you like. You might try making a
   design with them. You could also group
   the stamps according to their color, the
   pictures on them, or the countries they
   came from.

Amazing Fact

A one-cent stamp
made in British
Guiana in 1856 was
sold in 1980 for
$935,000. There is
only one known copy
of the stamp.